Copyright © 2024 Tess Whitehurst
Artwork © 2024 Jasmine Becket-Griffith

All rights reserved. Other than for personal use, no part of these cards or this book may be reproduced in any way, in whole or part, without the written consent of the copyright holder or publisher. This publication is intended for spiritual and emotional guidance only. The content is not intended to replace medical assistance or treatment. The views and opinions expressed by the author, both within and outside of this publication, do not necessarily reflect the views of the publisher.

Published by Blue Angel Publishing®
10 Trafford Court, Wheelers Hill,
Victoria, Australia 3150

info@blueangelonline.com
www.blueangelonline.com

Edited by Peter Loupelis and Jules Sutherland
Designed by Sunshine Connelly

Blue Angel® is a registered trademark
of Blue Angel Gallery Pty Ltd.

ISBN: 978-1-922574-17-6

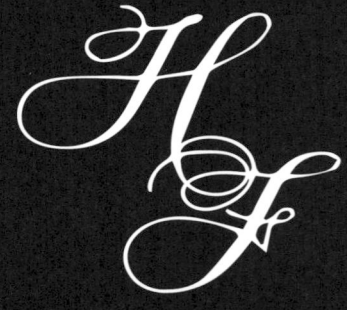

AN ENDLESS HALLOWEEN -7

HOW TO PREPARE YOUR DECK -9

HOW TO DO A READING -12

ABOUT THE AUTHOR -110

ABOUT THE ARTIST -111

THE CARDS

1. Owl Faerie -18
2. Candy Witch -20
3. The Wicked Witch's Hourglass -22
4. Lilith's Freedom -24
5. Light into Darkness -26
6. Second Spring -28
7. Work Your Magic -30
8. Cuddle the Dragon -32
9. Share the Cupcakes -34
10. Planetary Wisdom -36
11. Possum Faerie -38
12. Tiger Lily Nymph -40
13. Candy Moonbeams -42
14. Moon Moth -44
15. Voodoo in Violet -46
16. Hecate's Butterflies -48
17. Death Priestess -50
18. La Luna -52
19. Bone Bouquet -54
20. Hela's Chariot -56
21. El Corazón -58
22. Fierce Yōkai -60
23. Zombie Kitty & Queen -62
24. Leto's Temple -64
25. Listen to the Dead -66
26. La Catrina -68
27. Queen of Halloween -70
28. Conjure the Dragon -72
29. La Calavera -74
30. Empire of Bones -76
31. Santa Muerte -78
32. Fire Ritual -80
33. Chiaroscuro -82
34. Octopus Faerie -84
35. Ophelia's Ghost -86
36. Pumpkin Baby -88
37. Immortal Gaze -90
38. Pumpkin Thief -92
39. Will-o'-the-Wisp -94
40. Jack-o'-Lantern of Love -96
41. Medusa's Mysteries -98
42. Pumpkin Promise -100
43. Moon Mistress -102
44. Autumn Angel -104
45. Dracula's Heiress -106
46. Daughters of Night -108

AN ENDLESS HALLOWEEN

Everyone knows Halloween is a day of revelry: of costumes, candy, and wicked fun. But what everyone doesn't know is that Halloween is filled with profound and sacred spiritual power. It's a time when the veil between the worlds is thin — the worlds of human and faerie and, most famously, the worlds of the living and the dead.

Halloween is a cross-quarter day: an astronomical marker, astrological portal, and witches' sabbat that falls halfway between a solstice and an equinox — the Fall Equinox and Winter Solstice in the Northern Hemisphere and the Spring Equinox and Summer Solstice in the Southern.

For the northern half of the globe, Halloween coincides with its predecessors and roots: the pagan holiday of Samhain, the Mexican Día de los Muertos celebrations, and similar global celebrations of the harvest, deceased loved ones, and the realm of the dead.

In the Southern Hemisphere, Halloween coincides with the Celtic holiday and witches' sabbat of Beltane: the springtime festival that marks the moment when the faerie kingdom is closest and most accessible and when we can, therefore, most clearly sense and communicate with the fae.

In some traditions, the realm of the dead is the realm of the fae: they are one and the same. The faeries are none other than our spiritual counterparts on the other side. Naturally, some of these spirits are bright, beloved, and loving, while others are eerie, shadowy, and aloof. But it's not always clear cut — most spirits, much like those of us in the living realm, fall somewhere in between.

The Halloween Forever Oracle holds open the veil between the realms all year round. In the aura of this oracle, where every day is Halloween, you will find the guidance you seek and the answers you need. Delightfully sweet and spooky secrets will be revealed. Here in this never-ending Halloween, you will discover vital keys to happiness, joy, laughter, personal power, inner and outer healing, and all forms of success.

A glow-in-the-dark party invitation has arrived in your mailbox. Ghostly laughter beckons. Trick-or-treaters are knocking on your door.

Read on to learn how you can consult *The Halloween Forever Oracle* and discover the delicious and delightful confections that await within this endless All Hallows' Eve.

HOW TO PREPARE YOUR DECK

While you can certainly skip ahead to the next section and begin working with and receiving answers from your cards right away, performing a simple blessing ceremony will spiritually attune and supercharge your deck. Plus, it will be fun.

To bless your deck, begin by gathering the following:

- One black or orange candle, any size
- A lighter or matches
- Sweetgrass or copal incense (optional)
- One incense holder as needed (optional)
- Two little sweet treats, such as two gummy candies, two dried apple slices, or two miniature chocolate bars
- Your oracle deck (of course)

After dark on any night of your choosing, go somewhere quiet where you can be alone and undisturbed for at least 20 minutes or so. Light the candle and (if you'd like) the incense. Sit comfortably and settle in. Close your eyes and take a few deep, conscious breaths. Then continue to breathe naturally and deliberately until your mind feels centered and your body feels grounded and relaxed.

Call on the Divine in any way that feels best to you. For example, you might say:

Great Spirit, God/Goddess/All That Is, I call on you.

Thank you for surrounding me in the bright, golden-white, protective light of peace.

Envision a blinding sphere of golden-white light filling your body and surrounding you in a protective bubble of good energy and love.

Now, hold the deck in both hands. Say:

Faeries, spirits, and beloved dead, I invoke you. Otherworld, I call you. Bless this deck. Attune it to your wisdom and open my senses and intuition so I can receive your guidance through the magic of these images and words.

Envision, imagine, and feel the deck being filled with the light of faerie magic and spirit wisdom. Sense yourself being filled with this same light. Get the sense that you and the deck are resonating at the same frequency, so the messages that come through the deck will be naturally clear and apparent to you.

Bathe the deck in the incense smoke for a moment, then place it face down near the candle. Place one sweet treat on top of it and say:

I offer you this sweet as a token of my gratitude. Thank you.

Mindfully savor the other treat as you internalize the magic and attune even more powerfully to the spirits, the faeries, the sweetness of Halloween, and the living vibration of the deck.

Feel even more gratitude.

Now, extinguish the candle and incense. Leave the sweet on the deck overnight. In the morning or any time the following day, after unwrapping it (if it is wrapped), place it in a compost bin or bury it in the earth. Your deck is now ready for use.

HOW TO DO A READING

There are many ways you can work with this oracle deck. While you can certainly follow your intuition and make up your own rules, here are some helpful ideas and guidelines for getting started and making the most of this sacred, magical tool.

Whatever type of reading you're doing, you'll first want to ground and center your energy by relaxing your body and quieting your mind. To do this, sit comfortably, with your spine relatively straight. Close your eyes and take several deep, conscious breaths. Then allow your breathing to be natural while continuing to notice when you are breathing in and when you are breathing out. This will naturally bring your mind, body, and spirit into alignment in a relatively short amount of time.

Next, call on the Divine or the Infinite in a way that feels powerful to you. For example, you might simply say or think, *"Great Goddess, I invoke you,"* or *"Universal Wisdom, I call you."*

You may or may not want to light a candle and otherwise set the mood.

How to Do a General Reading

If you'd like, in the morning before you start the day, or as a prequel to your meditation or other daily spiritual work, you can do a general reading. This reading does not involve a specific question, but rather opens you up to whatever wisdom will most support you now.

To do a general reading, shuffle your deck. Stop whenever you feel like it. Cut the deck once or twice. Then take the first card off the top and turn it face up.

First, gaze at the image. Get your own impression as you allow yourself to simply appreciate the beauty of the card. Then, turn to the accompanying page in this guidebook and read the card description. Notice any words, phrases, or sentences that stand out to you. Relax and take your time as you soak in the guidance as it is written and unfolds within your mind. Breathe it in and set the intention to let your body and energy field also receive the guidance. Then, throughout your day, notice opportunities to apply the wisdom you've received.

How to Do a Reading on a Specific Topic

If you have a particular question, issue, or challenge about which you'd like to consult the oracle, first ground and center your energy as described above. Next, phrase your question in an open-ended way. In other words, instead of asking a 'yes' or 'no' question, ask a question such as the following:

- What do I need to know about _____?

- How can I best deal with _____?

- What guidance will help bring about the best possible outcome regarding _____?

- What would be the wisest approach to take with _____?

- What action or mindset will bring me the most peace [or success, abundance, etc.] in the situation with _____?

- What important wisdom will _____ help me learn?

If you'd like, write your question in a journal or notebook or simply speak it inwardly or aloud.

Next, shuffle the deck. When you feel ready to, stop. Then employ one of the following spreads.

1. *Werewolf Spread*

The Werewolf Spread is a simple yet comprehensive spread that will help you solve problems, tackle challenges, and see deeply into the true nature of your current transformation and change.

Take the first three cards off the top, and place them face up, left to right.

Card One — the waxing moon: the energy that is building and leading up to the transformation, culmination, or solution.

Card Two — the full moon: the full expression of the situation or challenge, how you are transforming, and how to best deal with it.

Card Three — the waning moon: the energies, issues, and challenges you are letting go of and are dissolving away.

2. *Pumpkin Spread*

The Pumpkin Spread is ideal for questions about communities: clubs, families, and group dynamics.

Take the first four cards off the top, and place them face up, left to right.

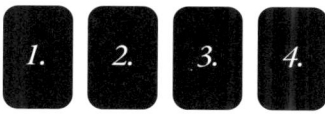

Card One — the seed: what has given birth to the challenge or issue, or where it began.

Card Two — the vine: the health, wellness, and interpersonal concerns related to the community or group.

Card Three — the fruit: the result of the teamwork or the culmination of the challenge, and how to best work with what's happening.

Card Four — the pie: what can you make from this challenge? What can you learn? What is the hidden potential for sweetness and enjoyment, and how can you bring it into form?

3. Faerie Witch Spread

The Faerie Witch Spread will help you see where and how to work your magic to affect the most favorable outcome for yourself and everyone concerned.

Take the first five cards off the top, arranging them face up, from left to right.

Card One — the present situation: what is happening and how you can understand it better.

Card Two — what you expect or desire: how you are presently imagining or hoping this will play out, and the energy you are projecting and swirling into the mix.

Card Three — your advice: how you can work your magic to transform this challenge or situation in the best and most helpful possible way.

Card Four — the shadow: hidden, concealed, or unexpected aspects to this question or challenge, and how you can bring them into the light.

Card Five — the outcome: what the result will be, and how you can move forward in the wisest and most empowered possible ways.

Now, go forth and play. While you can certainly request serious guidance on important questions, you will find the most success when you approach your intuitive work with the spirit of impish experimentation and frolicsome adventure. For Halloween asks us to see even the gravest issues and heaviest topics in sweet, playful, and childlike ways.

1. OWL FAERIE

*Luxuriate in this moment. Access clear divine guidance.
Come into the present moment, inhabit your senses,
and notice the wealth you already have.*

The owl faerie and her venerable companion remind you that you already have what you need. Your blessings and wisdom are only awaiting your recognition, appreciation, and attention.

Halloween coincides with the pagan holiday of Samhain, which is the last of three harvest festivals. The pumpkins have been gathered, so it's time to relax and celebrate the sweet results of all your hard work. When you appreciate the abundance that already surrounds you, you will magnify it and open the floodgates to your ever-increasing good.

If you're looking for direction, the owl faerie counsels you to look within and ask for help from the spirit realm. When you do so, be sure to relax and sensitize yourself to the beauty of the present moment. If you are patient and present, the wisdom you are seeking will naturally arise as an inner voice or a calm sense of certainty and crystal-clear inner knowing.

If you're asking about money or resources, the owl faerie wants you to savor the sweetness of the moment, and she points to all the riches you already have. By remembering all the ways you are already lucky and blessed, you will unblock the prosperous flow that is your divine right and natural state.

Dress in colors and textures that feel sumptuous and opulent to you. As you eat, revel in the taste of each delicious bite. Slow down and expand into the moment, without needing to hurry along to the next. As you let go of the desire for immediate answers or results, let your body relax and your lungs expand. This will align you with the harvest season, the silent resonance of ancient wisdom, and the sweet and opulent beauty of the now.

What you need, you have. What you seek is yours. Slow down, relax, pay attention, and allow it all to come to you in its own time and way.

2. CANDY WITCH

Be sweet. Be kind. Be loving.
Send out confectionary waves of blessings and goodwill.

The candy witch uses her sugary magic to create positive change in her life and the world. She urges you to do the same.

If you're inquiring about a person or relationship, conjure up a feeling of love, imagine it as a candy cloud, and mentally send it to everyone concerned. In much the same way that you would offer candy to any and all trick-or-treaters who may knock on your door, offer sweetness to everyone you encounter and anyone who crosses your mind.

Even though at times it will be appropriate to clearly set a boundary or firmly speak your truth, you can still offer universal love to all beings.

Being loving and sweet does not mean you should be a pushover or allow yourself to be mistreated. Contrary to conventional wisdom, standing up for yourself can coincide with understanding, generosity, and transcendent goodwill for all.

The candy witch's strength comes from her vulnerability and open heart. You too are being called to be both compassionate and powerful. So, stop for a moment. Close your eyes. Breathe, relax, and place a hand on your heart. Set the intention to be kind to yourself and surround yourself with love. Then radiate this love out into the world. Send it to your friends, your enemies, your acquaintances, and strangers. Send it across the surface of the planet, to all sentient beings. Then sense it coming back to you in wave after wave of delicious sweetness and light.

In addition to working on the level of energy and emotion, ask yourself: what can I offer? What can I give? How can I make the world a sweeter place?

In truth, we are all part of one consciousness. Being sweet to others means being sweet to yourself and vice versa. So, choose to cultivate harmony. Hold the vision of peace.

3. THE WICKED WITCH'S HOURGLASS

Be careful with self-constructed time limits and deadlines.
They may serve to sabotage or restrict your own success.
Release micromanagement and surrender to divine flow.

In the film version of *The Wizard of Oz*, the Wicked Witch imprisons Dorothy and then uses a magic hourglass to visually measure the time she has left to live. The irony is that in doing so, the witch sets in motion the events that lead to her own demise.

Don't make the same mistake now. For example, perhaps you have an age in mind by which you must reach a milestone or goal. It could be that you believe you are not really living until you are married, or own your own home, or make a certain amount of money. Or, perhaps, you are comparing yourself to others you perceive as living blessed or idyllic lives.

While structure, efficiency, and time sensitivity can at times be helpful and needed, you are being overly hard on yourself or others regarding time, and it is not serving you. You may be employing scare tactics or ultimatums to hurry things along or force things to look like you think they should.

So, take a moment to tune in. Close your eyes, relax, and get clear on how you have been wasting your energy in such ways. Even if it's not immediately obvious, with just a little willingness, you will know what this card is urging you to see.

Once you have clarity on your self-limiting behaviors and beliefs around time, be willing to let go of them. You can begin to free yourself by asking: what if everything is unfolding in perfect timing? What if I could release my impatience, envy, or desire to control or manipulate, and instead enjoy the moment, exactly as it is? What would that look like? How would it feel?

Ask the Divine for help with cultivating a more harmonious relationship with time. Choose to appreciate your life as it is now while staying awake to all the opportunities that arise.

4. LILITH'S FREEDOM

Wield your power. Refuse to be silenced or disenfranchised.
Rebel against oppression and the status quo.

Lilith is a primordial spirit in ancient Jewish and Mesopotamian mythology. Believed by some to be Adam's first wife, their relationship ended after she declined to be domesticated or tamed. A winged, taloned fire goddess who sparks uprisings and fuels revolutions, she has been called Lucifer's feminine counterpart.

In this image, Lilith wears garments fashioned from her broken chains. Her eyes burn with luminous fire. Behind her, a fierce angel stands ready to guard and guide you, and a lighted tunnel beckons you to step out of the abyss.

Perhaps you were raised with a cosmology or ideology that cast you in the role of sinner and threatened you with ideas of eternal damnation. But even if you weren't, you have been subjected to limiting cultural ideas about who you are or should be. For example, mainstream culture has historically shunned women for being anything other than cheerful and accommodating, shamed men for being sensitive or emotionally expressive, and cast judgment onto anyone who does not conform to binary and heteronormative models of gender and sexuality.

While you will undoubtedly benefit from refusing to be held back by such false and tiresome cultural tropes, this card may also point to a more situationally specific restraint you must break free from if you want to thrive. There may be a truth you need to speak or a bold action you need to take in your relationship, family, or workplace. It may feel risky to go against authority or potentially upset a loved one, but it is a risk you must take if you are to honor who you are. Even though you can't control other peoples' responses, you must speak up for what is right and take the actions that will set you free.

Lilith is very clear — break your chains and be yourself. Keep your own counsel, defend your independence, and claim your freedom.

5. LIGHT INTO DARKNESS

Brave the shadows of your psyche. Shine light onto your fears. Boldly wade into what you seek to escape or deny, and breathtaking beauty will bloom.

In a dark forest, the fae priestess in this image steps into a sacred spring. All around her, lush flowers grow, including primroses, chrysanthemums, begonias, morning glories, and poppies: symbols of courage, enjoyment, magical awakening, finding healing in dreams, and shining light in the darkness. She holds symbols of two of humanity's greatest fears: money and death.

What is your greatest fear? It could be poverty or wealth, failure or success, death or courageously showing up for life. It could also be any of these, in any combination, or it could be something more or less specific: a particular outcome or a general feeling of anxiety and unease.

Receiving this card indicates that you will benefit from shadow work now. That means getting honest about your fears, worries, and insecurities so you can stop running from them and look them squarely in the face. When you do this, you will overcome inertia, bust through blocks, and reclaim your courage. This will transform your position from disempowerment to personal authority.

If you're unsure what fear or insecurity this card refers to, grab a notebook and pen. Then freewrite (write without stopping) at least a half a page for each of the following prompts: whom do I most envy or resent, and why? What do these people have in common? And what quality might they share that I refuse to embody or admit?

If that doesn't give you the clarity you seek, or if you'd like to delve deeper, ask and answer: what monsters or villains in movies and books scare or fascinate me the most? What is it about them that unsettles or entrances me? How would it feel to bravely face these fears or see these qualities in myself?

Whatever you have been avoiding, look at it unflinchingly. Then offer it up to the Divine, ask for guidance, and bravely and gracefully proceed.

6. SECOND SPRING

Find the unique beauty in this stage of your life. Turn over a new leaf. Be delighted and surprised by this transformation into a wiser, more masterful, and more authentic you.

The fall faerie in this image embodies the Albert Camus quote, "[Autumn is] a second spring when every leaf is a flower." Her monarch butterfly wings indicate that she was a caterpillar faerie in the spring and summer of her life, crawling around in the dirt. Then she went through a confusing ordeal involving a cocoon, darkness, and excruciating pain. Now, at long last, she has emerged into the luminous colors of autumn. To top it all off, she has wings now, and can fly.

Like autumn leaves and butterfly wings, every new stage has its own fabulous charm. Youth has its pleasures, but so does age. The sun is dazzling, but so is the moon. A bright new morning is a joy, but so is the golden splendor of the late afternoon.

Recognize that you have wisdom, abilities, and opportunities now that you have not possessed in the past. It is easier for you to be kind to yourself now, for example, and to let yourself rest and take breaks so you can recharge and later emerge refreshed. You can take a longer view and access a more complete perspective now than you previously could.

How can you draw upon these changes to maximize your joy? It may be time to initiate a new project or direction, even if you previously believed it's too late for such an endeavor. In fact, if there's something your heart of hearts wants to try, now is the perfect time, for now you possess greater wisdom and mastery than ever before.

Even though you must say goodbye to the past, there is a brand new present to say hello to, which will unfold like butterfly wings and carry you up and away into the gorgeous autumn sky.

7. WORK YOUR MAGIC

Summon help from both seen and unseen realms. Proactively set your intentions and work your magic. Ask for and receive what you need.

———

The dragonfae witch in this image knows the outcome she desires, even if she doesn't quite know how to singlehandedly bring it into form. So, she is wisely invoking her skeleton allies for help while her beloved magical cat keeps her company and provides emotional support.

Follow her example by first clarifying what you would like to experience. If you're inquiring about a situation, what outcome would bring you the most satisfaction? If this is more of a general reading, what feeling or condition will bring you the most joy? State your objective, acknowledge your goal, and calmly clarify your desire.

Write your intention in the present tense in a journal or notebook, as if it's already true. Keep it simple, and include specifics and expansive emotions in your wording. For example, instead of writing, "I want a job I love, and I want to make plenty of money," you could write, "I love my job and it feels so empowering to make more than ____ per month." Take your time. Revise, rework, and fine tune this intention until it feels just right.

Now, light a candle or otherwise set an ambient mood. Relax and take some deep breaths. Speak your intention aloud. Earnestly and from your heart, ask your ancestors, angels, or spirit guides for help. Follow up with something like:

I know you can help me with this goal. I release it to you now. As I relax and trust, I promise to listen deeply for your guidance, so I know what actions will most effectively steer me toward my desired outcome. Thank you.

Feel as if you are handing over the whole situation to your allies. Do your best to embody the sensation that your intention is already manifested. Feel expansion and gratitude throughout your entire being.

Work your magic. Get clear on what you want, enlist your allies, relax, and trust that your desire is already on its way to you.

8. CUDDLE THE DRAGON

Adopt an animal friend or offer extra kindness and care to the one(s) you already have. Cherish your home and create a nourishing atmosphere for all who enter and dwell within.

The dragonfae in this image holds her beloved dragonling daughter with love and protectiveness. The jack-o'-lantern leers menacingly, magically safeguarding them from harm. The soft earth cradles them as the full moon basks them in the calm and healing radiance of the great Mother Goddess.

When you offer kindness, create coziness, and kindle the spark of love, you set a positive momentum in motion and construct a virtuous circle and feedback loop. In much the same way that giving or receiving affection stimulates the release of oxytocin—the warm, fuzzy hormone—into your bloodstream, maintaining and acting from the value of protective love vastly enriches the lives of everyone involved, including you.

That's why compassion and care are not solely altruistic. They are also priceless gifts to yourself, unlocking a deep sense of purpose, meaning, and joy.

So, ask yourself: how can I offer fierce love to another being now? How can I create a warm and inviting space for healing? How might proactive nurturing transform this situation for the better? How can simple kindness and open-hearted devotion help mend a broken heart, bolster a desired outcome, or repair a challenge or rift?

We all have a natural, intrinsic desire to love and to serve. The answer to your question is interwoven with this need. So, it might also be illuminating to ask yourself: how can I serve? How can I channel my talents toward the greater good? How can I be a beacon and bastion of unconditional support?

When you stop struggling, worrying, or attempting to control this situation by other means, and simply offer cuddling, companionship, or care, your whole outlook will transform and your ideal outcome will manifest.

9. SHARE THE CUPCAKES

Cook up some magic and spread it around. Generously give to loved ones or strangers. Commit random acts of kindness and offer your gifts to the world.

The lovely little bat faerie in this image has far more cupcakes than she can eat, yet she is hoarding them all for herself. In fact, she will reap much more enjoyment from her treasure if she shares it with others. That way, she will not only have plenty for herself, but she will also be investing in memories, relationships, and community, and setting in motion the endless boomerangs of blessings that result from generosity and compassionate interconnection.

If you feel insecure, you may attempt to compensate by shutting down and keeping everything to yourself. For example, loneliness begets loneliness when your isolation causes you to distrust others. Friendships can't blossom if you don't share your vulnerability or offer your loving support. Finances can't grow if you lock down your assets and refuse to wisely invest in your future and offer something of value to the world.

Admittedly, it can feel scary to put yourself out there. What if you invite people over for cupcakes and no one shows? Or what if they show but take the cupcakes and then don't express their appreciation or delight? The thing is, whether you're asking about career, finances, a relationship, or anything else, daring to be generous is the cost of doing business. One can never succeed without a brave willingness to try — and possibly feel the sting of rejection or failure.

This may be a message to throw a party, call a friend, donate to a cause you care about, or create something beautiful (such as a business, a charitable endeavor, or a work of art) and offer it to the world.

What you send out will return to you multiplied, but in a different form. Give away some of your cupcakes and you will receive wealth, laughter, companionship, a sense of belonging, and all that makes life worth living.

10. PLANETARY WISDOM

Examine your astrological aspects at work.
Interweave your intentions with planetary energies.
Find clarity and mastery by looking to the stars.

Here, we have a powerful witch holding the earth in her hands, flanked by wise incarnations of her very own self, attuning to the influences of Venus and Mars.

You too will benefit by sensitizing yourself to the astrology of this time. Whatever you're inquiring about is related to a current planetary position or transit. Look at the big picture: the cosmos and your unique place in the dance of the planets and stars. What sign is the Sun in today? And what about the Moon? Take advantage of the cosmic energies at play.

For example, if you want to manifest something, look at an astrological calendar and plan a ritual when the Moon is between new and full. You can also choose a time when the Moon will be in a sign related to your goal: like Libra for balance, Capricorn for focus, or Leo for fame and recognition. If you're experiencing friction at work, you could see what's happening with Mars. If you're asking about a relationship challenge, consider what Venus is up to.

Also, get a general picture of what's happening in the sky: is it eclipse season? What planets are retrograde? Are there any significant happenings that astrologers are writing articles about or discussing in their podcasts? Pay attention and you will find both answers and opportunities for growth.

You will also find great value in looking at your own chart, even if you've looked at it before — many websites offer you a free chart when you enter your birth information. Learn or give yourself a refresher on your Sun, Moon, and rising signs, as well as the signs and houses your other planets were in at the time of your birth.

The planets hold your answer. Look to the wisdom of the sky, and you will gain the perspective, guidance, and motivation you need.

II. POSSUM FAERIE

Look beyond the popular, conventional, and mainstream. Open your mind, dare to be different, and choose your allies according to your inner compass. Befriend the marginalized and the unfairly maligned.

Adorable, platinum-furred, pink-nosed possums are gentle, loyal, and kind. While many loathe and fear possums, the faerie in this image is their champion, and she receives great benefits from tending to the alliance she nurtures with her nocturnal tribe.

You are being called to stand up for an underdog or defend an ostracized group. It may be time to sing the praises of a previously unsung hero or publicly own your less popular opinions or traits.

Alternatively, this could be a message to let your silver hair grow out, to embrace your hair's inherent texture, to love your curves, to treasure your laugh lines or crow's feet, or to otherwise rock your natural beauty with pride. In a way, this is a continuation of the general message of this card because when you proudly embrace your less popularly celebrated traits, you will inspire others to do the same.

Conformity is boring. If we all molded ourselves to align with the mind-numbing opinions and standards of the day, we would never evolve — personally or as a culture. What's more, there is great enrichment and wisdom to be gained by listening to those who have previously been silenced, discounted, or denounced.

If you find yourself at a gathering of any kind, seek out the quiet and the shy. Ask them about themselves. Listen to what they have to say. If you feel quiet or shy, don't judge yourself for it. Love and approve of exactly how you feel. Send compassion to yourself and know you are not alone.

Give a voice to the voiceless. Offer a platform to those who have been silenced or ignored. Inspire courage in others and summon the audacity to share your uniqueness and shine your magical light.

12. TIGER LILY NYMPH

Cultivate confidence. Wield your queenliness.
Expect the best and keep your standards high.

In the Victorian language of flowers, the tiger lily represents the most positive aspects of pride. Tiger lily is also associated with wealth, prosperity, and royal authority.

The divine nymph in this image knows her worth: she wakes up every morning and revels in her regal presence and power. She is so divinely magnetic that she naturally attracts an endless stream of gifts, honors, compliments, windfalls, and lucky breaks. The gleaming brass fence and glowing wall of flowers in front of her symbolize her fabulous boundaries: she does not allow anyone to mistreat or devalue her. Her masterful eye makeup illustrates the time she takes and attention she pays to lovingly burnish her glory.

Be like the tiger lily nymph. Recognize your own majesty. Prioritize excellence. Spend time making your very existence feel luxurious. Take pride in who you are.

While confidence is an internal quality, there are external actions you can take to support this inner shift. Ask yourself what self-care behaviors will help infuse you with an abiding sense of pride. For example, your self-image can often benefit from consciously, lovingly tending to your wardrobe, makeup, nails, hair care, or interior design.

If you have been spending money without conscious attention to your financial wellness, you can increase your confidence by turning this behavior around. Monthly or weekly, take a good look at where your money is coming from and where it's going. If necessary, seek out more sustainable means of earning money. Make a plan for saving, investing, and responsibly paying off debts. No matter how long your past habits have been in place, you can always bring your full attention to your finances, replace negligence with presence, and take steps to nourish your long-term financial goals.

Shift into a more conscious, confident, and self-treasuring vibration now. You will immediately feel better, and you will quickly improve your luck. And, over time, you will attract ever-increasing levels of joy, prosperity, and success.

13. CANDY MOONBEAMS

*Summon and savor sweetness. Create your own luck.
Proactively turn your mood around.*

This Halloween faerie is conjuring up a vibe. With the help of her favorite candy and the full harvest moon, she is mustering up the ambiance of enchantment and creating the conditions for magic to occur.

If you are bored with life, it's your job to change that. If you feel that your magic has deserted you or that your life leaves a bitter taste on your tongue, you are the one you've been waiting for. Relax, look within, and find even one glowing ember of pleasure or sweet spark of inspiration. Then magnify it. Place your attention on it, tend to it, and fan its flames.

This faerie, for example, felt listless, empty, and down on her luck. Racking her brain for something that stoked her excitement for life, she thought of one simple thing: Halloween candy. It reminded her of carefree laughter, playfulness, and childlike joy. So, she surrounded herself with candy and savored it generously as she performed a spell for sweetness under the full harvest moon.

What's a simple action that stokes your own sense of spirited enjoyment? There may only be one thing you can think of right now that sounds even a little bit doable, and that's okay. Go with it. You may, perhaps, feel like everything seems dull except for baking cookies, listening to music, or calling a particular friend. Even if you don't feel excited about anything at all, push yourself just a little to beautify yourself or your home. Paint your nails, get your Halloween costume ready, try out a new hairstyle, clean, clear clutter, or decorate whimsically.

If you sit around waiting for things to change, you will only stay stuck and experience more of the same. So, find your own Halloween candy. Be proactive about finding, creating, and holding the space for excitement and delight. This will free up your inspiration, motivation, and intuitive knowing about how to proceed.

14. MOON MOTH

Get quiet. Steer clear of harshness. Be exceptionally gentle with yourself. Honor your sensitivity, take care of your energy, and act in accordance with your clear inner knowing now.

This moon moth faerie may be delicate, but she is also powerful, for she is attuned to the wisdom of the Great Goddess and the subtle frequencies of the spirit realm. She has appeared to remind you that you also have these abilities, but to hear your guidance, you must first relax and spend some quiet time alone to purify and reset yourself: mind, body, and spirit.

While there's nothing wrong with having a full schedule or enjoying rich foods and celebratory beverages, when these behaviors are too frequent and you don't take enough downtime to heal, cleanse, and recharge, your intuitive and psychic abilities will take a hit. But remember that it's perfectly natural to go in and out of balance throughout your life experience. So, there's no need to judge yourself when this happens. Instead, you can simply notice and take steps to remedy this condition now.

This is likely a message to cancel plans and carve out some time in your schedule for relaxation, meditation, rest, and attentive self-care. It is also quite possible that you will benefit from taking a break from too much sugar, alcohol, or other substances that, in excess, can block your connection to Spirit. Furthermore, you can help purify and reset your vibration by removing clutter, cleaning, and clearing the space in your home with chimes, bells, the smoke from ethically sourced dried palo santo or sage, a mister of rose water, or an aromatherapeutic space-clearing mist.

You will most certainly benefit from fine tuning your chakras and energy field. You can do this by performing a chakra-clearing or energy-healing meditation, or receiving a reiki healing or other energy work.

You are a channel of divine wisdom and healing. Relax, tend to your wellness, and then listen deeply. This will realign you with divine orchestration and flow.

15. VOODOO IN VIOLET

Channel your hurt and anger into art.
Create something inspiring out of your pain.
Let success be your revenge.

It appears someone has mistreated you or a loved one, or that you are otherwise experiencing reactive heartbreak or rage. But instead of seeking retaliation through direct punishment, you will find even greater satisfaction when you direct your emotion toward self-betterment and creative self-expression.

This dragonfae beauty was betrayed by someone she had previously trusted. And despite her natural skill in the practice of voodoo, she did not waste an ounce of energy on magically affecting harm. Instead, she used her heartbreak as fuel to create a whole line of artistic voodoo dolls. She eventually amassed so many that she decided to open a shop in the French Quarter of New Orleans. Now, she can barely keep up with the demand. While her ex-partner passes by her shop frequently and looks longingly at her through the windows, she has magically barred him from entry and has, in fact, blocked him from contacting her at all.

She rarely gives him a thought. She has far better things to do with her time.

Now, you must use your own challenge as fuel to propel you up and out of sadness and into triumph. Make excellence your goal and refuse to be discouraged or deterred. Like this violet-eyed entrepreneur who is now the toast of Bourbon Street, find the glorious fortune hidden within your seeming setback, and make your former tormentors and detractors wake up every morning cursing the day they forsook your alliance or broke your trust.

Whatever you're feeling, honor it. But don't give away your power to the thoughts, opinions, or behaviors of others. Be your own champion. Be strong. Burnish your beauty, maximize your prospects, and show the whole world just how magnificent you are.

16. HECATE'S BUTTERFLIES

This is both an ending and a beginning. Positive transformation is afoot. Let go of the old, transcend your fear, and welcome this powerful, empowering change.

Hecate is the goddess of death and the crossroads. While many fear her, she is revered and honored by those who are wise. Here, she appears in her truest form: both ancient and timeless, unspeakably old but with a luminous power that stokes her ageless glow. In one hand, she's holding a milkweed pod to nourish her butterflies and fuel their metamorphosis and migration. With the other hand, she's offering you the key that will open the door to your own sacred transformation and journey.

Hecate knows you've been navigating rough waters, under a stormy sky. But she assures you that you haven't been doing so in vain. In fact, you've come to a point of incredible potential. So acknowledge your suffering, knowing it has led you to greater wisdom, opportunity, and success.

If you're currently experiencing grief of any kind, feel your feelings fully, and let Hecate comfort you. She is ushering whomever or whatever you have lost into the light-filled realm of renewal and rebirth. As past conditions transform, so do you. As pain carves its mark into your being, so does your capacity for joy increase. Every single butterfly has experienced profound confusion and pain, without which they could never have gained their wings.

Don't fear change, but don't negate your tender or turbulent feelings as you move through life's inevitable turning points. Allow it all to coexist. Grief is a natural expression of love. Tragedy is the storm that will make the milkweed grow.

Hecate says: if you don't see the blessings in your current situation quite yet, look harder. Mourn your losses and breathe into your sorrow. And remember that every challenge contains a seedpod of positive change.

17. DEATH PRIESTESS

Say goodbye to past conditions. Refuse to suffer foolishness and fools. Proactively banish fear, disempowerment, and stagnation.

The death priestess encourages you to destroy unhealthy habits, dissolve anxious thought patterns, and demolish conditions that have been holding you back.

For many, death is the source of one's deepest and most desperate fears. But here, death is the ultimate cleanse: a decisive and transformational power that clears away the old and makes room for the new.

The death priestess's eyes radiate pure power and the emerald and rubies at her throat symbolize prosperity, passion, and verdant life. The plague doctor over her left shoulder indicates that your current situation cannot continue as it has been. Over her right shoulder, you can see Death himself in the distance calmly riding his horse. The miniature skeletons and plague doctors dancing around the priestess show that what may seem like a loss is in fact cause for celebration, for you are saying hello to exciting new conditions as you say goodbye forever to something that needs to go.

If you're unsure what this card may be telling you to banish, cleanse, or release, look deeper. What doesn't feel right to you anymore, or never did in the first place? Or what had to fall away for something new to be born? There may be a boundary you need to set or a truth you need to speak. Sometimes you need to facilitate an ending to open the way to the beautiful future you crave.

This might also be a message to let go of something on the mental or emotional plane. If you want to experience freedom, there may be an old paradigm, pattern, behavior, habit, or story you must refuse to entertain for one moment more.

Powerful alchemy is at work. From dead wood and brittle bones, bright flames will burn. Be brave. Willingly let go of the old and step into the new.

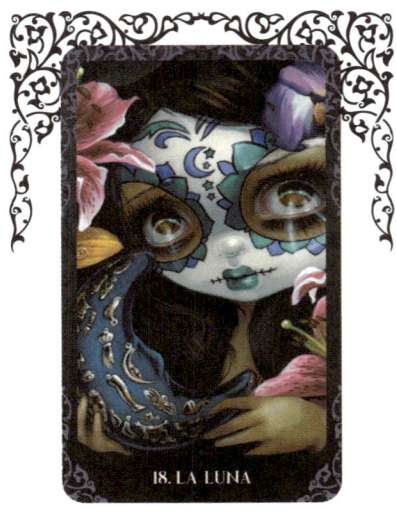

18. LA LUNA

Relax and receive. Revel in your considerable blessings. Cultivate everyday beauty and luxuriate in the little things.

Be like the moon, who quietly absorbs and gently radiates the golden light of the sun, easily attracting good fortune and effortlessly conferring inspiration and magic upon all who gaze at her luminous face.

Día de los Muertos, the Mexican 'Day of the Dead', coincides with Halloween, but its origins are far older, reaching back thousands of years. Here we have a gorgeous little *bruja* (witch) observing this ancient holiday. She is gazing at the moon, surrounded by lilies and irises (blooms sacred to the Divine Feminine), holding a moon covered in magical charms known as *milagros*.

Notice that she holds the moon gently. She does not grip it tightly, for she knows there is great power in relaxation and ease. In her stillness, she is open to the healing and empowering light of the moon and the delicious fragrance of the velvety flowers that flank her. In gazing upward, she releases attachment to certainty and trusts that her life's unfolding is governed perfectly by the moonlight and the music of the spheres.

Similarly, though it may seem counterintuitive, if you are to manifest your goals and achieve your aims, you must temporarily stop striving. You have already done the work. Your continued tension is keeping your desires at bay. When you stop holding on too tightly, you will allow your most desirable and magical outcome to unfold.

It's great to get clear on your dreams and desires, to take action as you feel guided, and to clearly state your intentions to the Goddess and the moon. But at some point, you must quieten your mind and luxuriate in your senses, so you can awaken to all the blessings of the moment and the magic can flow in and propel you forward into your glorious new stage.

The Goddess yearns to bless you with all that you desire. So relax, be still, stop seeking and striving, and allow all good things to come to you.

19. BONE BOUQUET

*Be fearless. Face and transcend your worries.
Let even death inspire you to live fully and fearlessly,
and to luxuriate in the beauty surrounding you now.*

Among human fears, death is the deepest and most profound. But when you live attempting to sidestep the truth of your inevitable and unpredictable end, your life will be half-lived. In fact, the certainty of death is a gift. If you allow it, it will infuse each moment of your life with incredible meaning and love.

Imagine you are on your deathbed, looking back over the moments of your life. How would your perspective shift? What would you change about how you are approaching your current situation or challenge?

What would you do more of, what would you do less of, and what would you stop doing altogether? What would you try? How would you treat others? How would you treat yourself?

While death is indeed an ending of a kind, it is more of a comprehensive and sweeping change. And while there are always sad aspects to it, it is not the straightforward tragedy it is made out to be. It is perhaps more accurate (and certainly more empowering) to think of it as the ultimate adventure.

Death allows us to see that life as a human on earth is a beautiful gift. It has its ups and downs, of course. It unfailingly presents you with both incredible sorrow and ecstatic moments of joy. But it is always something to be treasured and savored. Our unknown expiration date makes life even more precious and worthwhile.

Even though no living being can tell us plainly what death will be like, those who have gotten close say they have entered a realm of pure love and light, where they see clearly that, in fact, they were in that realm all along.

You are an eternal, luminous, divine soul, bathed in light. So, live fully and courageously. Embrace the reality of death and transcend all the fears that have been holding you back.

20. HELA'S CHARIOT

Release attachment to status. Simply be who you are, without apology or embellishment. While we all have weaknesses and strengths, our fundamental worthiness is the same.

Hela is the Norse goddess of death: keeper of souls and queen of the afterlife. She sometimes appears as a beauty, sometimes as a corpse, and sometimes as a bilateral hybrid of half-beauty/half-corpse. Here we see her in her loveliest form, riding in her bone chariot, surveying her underworld realm.

No one escapes Hela. It might be today, it might be tomorrow, and it might be in ten or twenty or fifty years. But we all have an appointment with the goddess of death. None of us are getting out of here alive. This awareness is the ultimate equalizer. While our social-obsessed human brains will always seek to quantify and qualify our status, in the end we are alike. We will all turn to dust and blow away.

Let this be an indisputable reminder of your equality. While you are still here, you have a right to speak up, be yourself, express your feelings and ideas, and thrive. Let it also be a reminder to respect these identical rights in each of your fellow humans, regardless of their race, religion, gender, sexuality, degree of wealth, level of education, political beliefs, or any other categorization or made-up marker of worth.

When you heed Hela's wisdom, your perspective will shift. You'll feel freer and clearer. You'll make new friends and enlist new allies you previously may have overlooked. You'll naturally propel yourself up and out of your challenge, and the winds of change will gently blow in and carry you to your most ideal destination.

As a human, it is natural to unconsciously imagine that the rule of death does not apply to you. But Hela is indifferent to your conceit. Look into her eyes. Receive her message. And be wise.

21. EL CORAZÓN

*Heal your heartbreak. Open your heart to love.
Take steps to support the physical wellness of your heart.*

Here we have a beautiful little *bruja* (witch), cradling a heart adorned with *milagros* (charms) for emotional and physical wellness. Lilies and irises, flowers of eternal life, divine support, and energetic healing surround her. Her golden-brown eyes radiate peace.

This is a clear message to tend to your heart. Place one or both hands there now. Close your eyes. Relax, breathe, and connect with your emotional center.

What does your heart say? What does it want? What does it need? If there is pain or worry there, breathe into it. Have compassion with yourself. Offer up your fearful thoughts to the divine. Say a prayer for courage. Reassure yourself that you are safe, you are loved, and you are more than equal to whatever may arise.

Whatever you're asking about, your heart knows what to do. Whatever you're dealing with, your heart holds both the answer and the cure.

It's possible that you will feel guided to seek therapy, to have a heart-to-heart talk with a loved one, or to make a doctor's appointment to assess the wellness of your physical heart. It might be time to get yourself flowers, or to light a candle on your altar and ask for the healing, courage, and guidance you need. Perhaps you'll feel inspired to reduce or mitigate stress through relaxation, time off, or a creative outlet. You may want to add more vegetables to your diet or cardio to your exercise routine to bolster the strength of your heart.

Wearing a bloodstone, aventurine, garnet, ruby, or rose quartz pendant over your heart would be an excellent way to strengthen your connection to your heart center, and it will help activate your intuition about where else to start and what to do next.

Tend to your heart as you feel guided, and you will succeed. Be loving to yourself and everyone concerned, and you will find peace.

22. FIERCE YŌKAI

Raise your frequency. Purify your vibration.
Call upon protective allies in the spirit world.

This gorgeous geisha is flanked by her supernatural two-tailed cats, known as *bakeneko*. A *kirin* (unicorn-like creature) is lightly and gracefully perched on her *shamisen* (stringed instrument).

While the geisha purifies her energy and the energy around her with the mellifluous sound of her music, her friends the *yōkai* (supernatural entities) keep all threatening and challenging energies at bay. The cats are known to seek immediate revenge for cruelty, and *kirins* are so loving and pure that anyone who harbors selfish motives or an intention to harm will be instantly incinerated while in their presence.

You, too, can summon such protective entities and benevolent energies to work in the invisible world on your behalf. For example, you might call on angels, deceased loved ones, or simply invoke and surround yourself in a sphere of divine white light.

Or, if you feel guided, you could strike up a relationship with fiercely positive animal spirits like the ones pictured here. While *kirin* and *bakeneko* are from Japanese folklore, similarly protective beings appear in the mythology of many cultures.

This card is a loving reminder to keep yourself safe in both seen and unseen realms. While it appears there is a hazard present or a line is being crossed, you need not allow this to continue for one moment more.

Even if the situation is not physically or spiritually dangerous, it has compromised your confidence and is undermining your power.

Chances are good you already know what this card is referring to, so in addition to calling on divine support, set boundaries as appropriate in the physical world: cancel your date, block someone from contacting you, add an extra layer of security to your home, stop oversharing, or take a step back and enforce a less intimate level of connection or trust.

Calmly, confidently, and lovingly reclaim your power and call on divine support to bolster your spiritual immunity. Take care of yourself swiftly and decisively. All the while, fear nothing — and you will soon find you indeed have nothing to fear.

23. ZOMBIE KITTY & QUEEN

Draw upon your scrappy resilience and hard-won wisdom. You've been through a lot, but you're still here. Your scars (whether visible or invisible) are not blemishes, but badges of honor.

Like this striking zombie and her adorable zombie kitty, let go of who you were and be proud of who you are. As challenging as it may have been, you cannot change the past, so you might as well acknowledge it, own it, and claim all the blessings and wisdom hidden within it. Accepting what is includes accepting what was. Once you come out of opposition to the present moment and all that has led up to it, you are free to rise on the stepping stones of your prior incarnations and ordeals.

It's possible you have been perceiving yourself as 'damaged goods', or seeing your former challenges as unsurpassable roadblocks to living your best life. While it's important to feel your painful feelings about what has transpired in the past, there is also a time to release and rewrite the old stories holding you back and keeping you stuck. Now is that time.

You need not forgive or forget, but you do need to look closely at the hidden blessings you have gained by going through the challenges that have befallen you. You are not as innocent or as trusting as you once were; this is true. But your newfound strength has burnished your magnificence in a different way. Lean into this strength and fully embody the profound beauty of your indomitable spirit.

No matter what has happened to you in the past, you can always be free, live happily, and be proud of who you are. You are not dead — you are only transformed. In this new form, you will find an inner fortitude you never could have foreseen.

So open the lid of your casket and scratch your way out of the soil. Now is your time to rise.

24. LETO'S TEMPLE

Protect your pack. Draw upon the support of your beloved family or friend group. Lend a helping hand to one or more loved ones in need.

While the goddess Leto, mother of Artemis and Apollo, is often considered a minor player in the Greek pantheon, she was likely worshipped as the great Mother Goddess in ancient Lykia. Leto is a wolf goddess who occasionally shape-shifts into a wolf, and it's no coincidence that Lykia (now part of modern Turkey) means 'wolf land'.

Devotees called on Leto for family protection, particularly for mothers and children. But she presides not just over birth and life, but also over death: she and her etheric wolfpack guard newly departed souls, lovingly ushering them to the afterlife. This aligns with the wolf's role as psychopomp: mediator and guide between the realms of the living and the dead.

Leto says: your actions can be more helpful than you know. By simply stepping in to assist a loved one or a group of loved ones in a time of need, the effects of your good deeds will reverberate for ages and generations to come. So, look closely and discover one or more ways to support your family, friend group, or community now.

Perhaps someone could use your help packing up and loading a moving van. You may find a volunteer opportunity to support local families or children in need. If you know a neighbor is having a hard time, you might bake them some cookies. Or your contribution could be as simple as calling a friend to check in.

This may also be a message to receive support from family, friends, or your community. Much like wolves, humans are communal animals. The 'lone wolf' does not generally thrive, which is why in nature, that archetype is more of the exception than the rule.

Remember that humans love to be of service: it's how we are wired. So, by receiving, you also give. Just as when you give, you also receive. It's time now to strengthen and add momentum to this virtuous circle of support.

25. LISTEN TO THE DEAD

One or more of your ancestors or deceased loved ones wants to be of assistance. Still your mind and pay attention. Listen deeply to what they are communicating.

You have a truly countless number of ancestors who no longer walk this earth in living human form. There may also be a relative or friend you knew in life who is present as a helper for you on the other side. Honor your ancestors and deceased loved one(s) now by consciously attuning to their guidance and welcoming the wisdom they want to impart.

Take meaningful action that demonstrates your love and willingness to connect. If you can, visit the graves of ancestors or deceased loved ones. Bring them flowers. Sweep or spruce up their monuments as needed. And most importantly, spend quiet time with their spirit(s) in meditation and contemplation.

As an alternative, or in addition, you might create an altar to your ancestors and deceased loved one(s). Place pictures or mementos that remind you of them, along with candles, flowers, and perhaps foods or beverages they once enjoyed. As you sit in silence before your altar, call up an inner connection to your non-physical friend(s). Feel your love for them and their love for you and employ it as a bridge of light that connects you to their living spirit(s) on the other side.

If you're asking about a specific issue or challenge, there is an ancestor or deceased loved one who wants to provide you with loving support as its outcome unfolds. For example, if you're inquiring about money, a financially savvy grandparent may have just the advice you need. And, as you consciously and deliberately work with this grandparent and remember to ask for their help, they will pull strings and grant favors that can help make your path easy, breezy, and fun.

Enlist the spirits. Awaken to magic. Allow your etheric allies to help you manifest the success you desire.

26. LA CATRINA

26. LA CATRINA

Adorn your body. Take pride in how you look. Let your outer appearance be an expression of your inner beauty.

La Catrina is the well-dressed feminine skeleton woman often portrayed and emulated in Día de los Muertos celebrations in Mexico and elsewhere. Her name means something like 'stylishly adorned woman'. Here, we see a stunning butterfly faerie in costume as La Catrina. Notice how her hair, makeup, accessories, and clothes are lovingly chosen and artfully assembled to beautiful effect.

While wardrobe and cosmetic choices are sometimes assumed to be shallow and frivolous concerns, this assumption does not reflect the ultimate truth. While we can indeed become overly fixated on how we look in such a way that we lose touch with our authentic depth, we can also consciously leverage our aesthetic choices to live with more satisfaction, connection, and joy.

You are going to get dressed and take care of your body anyway, and how you appear is literally how you 'show up'. Whether you like it or not, fashion, style, and haircare are inescapable, non-verbal forms of self-expression. So, you may as well make a ritual out of your self-care practices by approaching them with mindful presence. You may as well communicate to yourself and others that you value yourself and regard your body as a precious and priceless gift, worthy of attentive adornment and care.

While caring for and decorating your body may not seem relevant to your inquiry, remember that everything is connected. How you feel makes all the difference in how you are treated and behave. When you feel luxurious, you will attract wealth. When you feel worthy, you will teach others to treat you with respect.

Don't underestimate the magical powers of colors, patterns, materials, accessories, and scent. Used with intention, they can positively affect you on all levels, which will in turn positively impact every aspect of your life.

27. QUEEN OF HALLOWEEN

You are the queen, and you must lead.
Unapologetically embrace your role as boss.
Hold fast to your vision and don't hesitate to lay down the law.

———————

The Queen of Halloween reminds you of your goddess-given authority to establish and maintain the conditions you desire.

This may be a message to set boundaries in a relationship or group or a nudge to pursue and accept a leadership role at work or in your community.

You are the one that determines how you are treated. You must teach others what you expect and what you will and will not abide. Some will respect your guidelines, and others will not. This will clearly illustrate who does and does not belong in your life or your inner circle of camaraderie and trust.

You are likely being presented with an opportunity to lead. This role could be evident to you now, or it could be something that will reveal itself when you declare your willingness to be a conduit for divine leadership. Consult your inner wisdom and be honest: do you sense that you have a strong and positive inner vision that could serve as a roadmap for governance? Close your eyes and relax. Let yourself know how the Goddess is lovingly asking you to be the boss.

This may be a sign to run for political office, or to apply for or accept a job that involves guiding and managing others.

Gaze at the Queen of Halloween. Notice her confidence and sense her no-nonsense approach to leadership and life. Adopt her attitude as your own. Take her posture for a moment and imagine you are sitting on your throne. Feel your queenliness in your body and let it radiate it from your face. Then you will know exactly what this card is telling you to do.

There are times when it is appropriate to be a follower, and to go along with what others dictate or expect. This is not one of them. Wield your power audaciously and embrace your role as queen.

28. CONJURE THE DRAGON

Conjure up your confidence. Find creative and magical ways to coax out your brightness and boldness. Even if you feel shy or unsure, playfully shore up your courage and know that you are safe.

———————

Even though this beautiful dragonfaerie feels worried and insecure, she has summoned her power in the form of the dragon ally she carries in front of her heart. By imagining her bold positivity as a separate dragon ally or fetch, she has changed her circumstances and prospects for the better. She has emboldened herself to face her fears so she can triumph and thrive.

In just the same way, you are far more influential and capable than you feel. Even if these qualities feel woefully out of reach, you can magically bring them in anyway by closing your eyes, relaxing, and calling on the bright-red dragonling spirit that is, in fact, your very own self-assurance and unflagging positivity. While this spirit is somewhat metaphorical, it is also a literal part of you. By envisioning your confidence as a happy little dragon you carry in your arms, you make it more accessible, instantly. It is simply a way of relating to yourself that will help you actualize and wield your power.

What is your dragonling's name? What does it feel like to hold your little fireball in your arms? Work with this clear inner vision and let your playful experimentation open the door to your success.

In the spirit of this lighthearted approach, also look for ways to boost your chutzpah through what you wear and how you adorn yourself. For example, you will certainly feel and behave differently if you wear big black boots, sparkly makeup, or a brightly colored coat. As Halloween often reminds us, the costumes we wear bring out and enhance the inner qualities that align with how we outwardly appear.

Your confidence is there for you. It is simply a matter of creatively drawing it out. Play around with inner and outer strategies until you find the formula that works.

29. LA CALAVERA

See beyond the physical reality. Know yourself as eternal. Be fully present and live gracefully between the worlds of spirit and form.

Here we have a gorgeous little *bruja* (witch), holding a *calavera* (artistic skull). Her liquid eyes gaze through the veil of time to perceive infinity. In other words, she sees beyond the fleeting illusion and into the permanent truth. She knows herself and all other souls to be immortal, indestructible frequencies of power and light.

Address your day-to-day concerns without getting overly mired or enmeshed in them. They are temporary. They will pass, just as concerns from past eras in your life are gone forever, never to return. Similarly, whatever may arise in the future is something you can deal with then.

So let go of past and future and discover the limitless peace here for you now.

Shifting your perspective to the present moment and eternal reality will empower you to be more adept at dealing with your day-to-day problems and challenges, not less. For example, when you know down to your bones that you are only walking this planet in a physical body for a brief and unknowable span of time, it becomes less stressful to manage your finances, or to have an uncomfortable but necessary conversation with someone you love. When you release undue stress and anxiety around the little things, it becomes easier to hear your intuition about dealing with all the things in the healthiest and most sustainable ways.

Breathe deeply and relax your body and mind. Listen to silence and become aware of space. Sense your presence as a bright and buoyant quality of divine wisdom and light. Lift your perception up and out of the crown of your head and see the big picture. Then drop back into your body and feel your shoulders sink, your face soften, and your belly unclench.

You are vast and powerful: one with everything. So, patiently, reverently, move forward, and let eternal wisdom light your way.

30. EMPIRE OF BONES

You are a product of countless ancestors and billions of years of evolution. Vast wisdom floods and is encoded within your every cell. Draw upon the ancient whispers of all those who have contributed to your existence.

You are the culmination of a truly unknowable number of lineages: genetic, spiritual, and intellectual. All these flows of energy and information uniquely coalesce to comprise, define, enliven, and guide you.

If you consider just one of your grandparents, you can likely see that many of their experiences, talents, habits, and perspectives contributed to your own. But if you consider their parents, and then their parents, and then their parents before them, you will see that your origins are so ancient and so vast, you cannot even begin to conceptualize them. And yet, they hold precious keys to healing deeply and living with mastery and ease.

Draw upon the wisdom of your ancestors, the elders in your spiritual lineage, or the pioneers in your cherished discipline or craft. Recognize and foster the strengths and strategies they have passed along to you. And simply set the intention to connect with their power.

There are things you know, and know how to do, that come from these ancient currents of wisdom and light. Claim these talents. Acknowledge their origins and give thanks for all the many blessings they bestow. For example, you may have a way with herbs, a connection with crystals, or a talent for reading tea leaves or attuning to the stars. Perhaps color speaks to you, or you are a math or science whiz, or you have a sense for speaking words of comfort or sending healing energy through your hands.

If you relax, look within, and invoke the ancient wisdom that is your birthright, you will discover you already know what action or path to take. Notice your talents and proclivities. And let the sage expertise of the ages naturally flow to you and through you, lighting and guiding your way.

31. SANTA MUERTE

You must change your circumstances swiftly, utterly, and decisively. Powerful magic is required. Be clear on what you want, and then petition Santa Muerte for support.

Santa Muerte literally means 'Saint Death'. She is the Great Goddess and the Grim Reaper combined. She is both terrifying and compassionate, remorseless and full of love. Her power is unrivaled, transcending human values, morals, and law.

When you invoke Santa Muerte, you must not do so lightly. Obtain an image of her: a prayer candle, statue, printed image, or postcard will all suffice. Then create an altar to her. It can be simple or elaborate, provided it includes her image, at least one candle and an offering, such as fresh (never wilted) flowers, incense, fruit, hard alcohol, cigarettes, or candy.

Light the candle. Then relax, breathe deeply, and center your mind. Say:

Santa Muerte, beloved Saint Death, lady of my heart, I invoke you. Illuminate me with your wisdom and power. I ask that you help me with … [share what you need from your heart, being very clear on your desired outcome].

I thank you for helping to bring about this outcome by … [date].

Next, clearly state what additional gift you will offer Santa Muerte when your petition is fulfilled by the specified date. She especially appreciates bouquets of fresh white roses placed in a cemetery and entire bottles of tequila or whiskey, poured out in her name on the earth.

Now, thank Santa Muerte. Feel gratitude and thank her heartily. Light her candle once daily until your request is granted. Then be sure to follow through on your promise to offer her that additional gift.

Do not ignore this message. Be proactive and resolute so you can bring about the necessary change. With Santa Muerte's help, go beyond all fear and waste no time transforming your circumstances according to your will.

32. FIRE RITUAL

Throw your old heartaches and struggles on the fire and watch them burn. Energetically purge all traces of a past relationship or conflict. Feel your painful feelings until they are consumed and destroyed in their very own flames.

This sweet little faerie has been burned: betrayed, insulted, or emotionally abused. But instead of extinguishing the flames of her anguish, she is consciously channeling them toward incinerating the conditions and purifying the memories that have caused her heart to break.

Breathe deeply now, letting your full inhales and exhales fan the emotional flames in your belly and heart. While it may seem counterintuitive to breathe into the pain, the fire will not burn forever. In time, it will work its transformational alchemy, establishing lightness where there was heaviness and freedom where there may have once seemed to be a trap.

If you've recently ended a relationship, go through all your belongings and photos. Donate, destroy, or delete anything that is a reminder of or gift from your former partner or friend. This is not to show contempt for the love you have shared, but to release and transform your feelings in a healthy way. In getting these things out of your life, you will help free yourself from any of this person's lingering domination or sway.

Next, perform a fire ritual. Safely build a fire in a fireplace or firepit, or simply find yourself a cast iron cauldron or pot. Write a or draw on paper a symbol or description of what you would like to purify and transform. Crumple it up and burn it in the cauldron or throw it on the flames. Breathe deeply and feel the physical and emotional effects of this healing ritual as you watch it burn.

Extinguish the fire or let it burn out naturally. If you burned your paper in a cauldron or pot, wait until there's no trace of fire or smoke, and flush the ashes down the toilet or pour them down the drain.

Find cleansing renewal through the fire element and rediscover your natural joy.

33. CHIAROSCURO

Release black-and-white thinking and overcome the us-against-them mentality. Acknowledge the gray areas and look for the blessings in challenges. Transcend oversimplification, perceive the power in polarities, and see the complex beauty in yourself, others, and the world.

No one is all wicked or all good. We are all a complex interplay of the full spectrum of feeling, motivation, and experience.

The Wicked Witch herself is not entirely wicked, just as Glinda the Good is far from completely good. In fact, their fates and identities are so interwoven, without one, the other could not be fully herself. It is almost as if they are one being, narratively separated into two.

Chiaroscuro is an Italian word that literally translates to 'light-darkness'. It describes art and film that draw upon an intricate interplay of deepest darkness and brightest light. After all, without darkness, we could not perceive the light, and the brightest light casts the most profound shadow.

In some significant way, you have been seeking to oversimplify. You may be labeling or perceiving another person, yourself, or an entire situation in a way that leaves no room for subtlety, complexity, or depth. Perhaps you see someone as simply 'evil' or 'bad', or imagine there is no possible redeeming quality or blessing in a particular challenge. On the other hand, you may be mistakenly believing or wanting to believe that someone is an absolute angel — or you may choose to see your behavior as permanently beyond reproach.

Life is not a fairytale or a cartoon. It does not contain unredeemable villains or hearts of solid gold. Even the most desirable outcomes contain their challenges, just as even the most grievous tragedies offer us precious blessings and boons.

Life is a chiaroscuro, and if you want to experience it fully and masterfully, you must see it as such. Commit to the journey. Expect gray areas and appreciate the interplay of both darkness and light. Admire strengths, forgive weaknesses, and surrender to the Great Mystery.

34. OCTOPUS FAERIE

Draw upon your creative intelligence and ability to outsmart and possibly even deceive. It may benefit you to pretend to blend in, or to temporarily hold the shape of something you aren't. Like the octopus, be patient, stealthy, and wise.

This faerie is a shape-shifter: sometimes she manifests as an octopus, and other times as a lovely little goth girl. In either case, her appearance is even more fluid: she can be seen in many ways and through many lenses, depending on what will most benefit her at any given time.

Octopi are soft and sensitive creatures, making it necessary and natural for them to protect themselves in unique and inventive ways. They are intelligent, fluid, and adaptable, with exceptionally large and capable brains.

Now you must be like the octopus. Don't take the obvious path, don't draw attention to yourself, and don't act before thoroughly thinking things through. While deception is often not the most honorable tack, there are times when you must employ intrigue or subterfuge for your own safety or to effectively change your situation for the better.

For example, if you're working a job you dislike, this may be a message to do your best to persevere for a bit longer, pretending to fit in while you prepare for your next career move. Or, if you know or suspect you need to leave a problematic partnership, this is likely a nudge to map out your escape route, talk with trusted advisers and friends, and secretly arrange for travel and lodging before you announce your plans to leave.

In any case, be sure to listen, research, and observe before acting, and do your best to fly under the radar to achieve your aim. Others will share more with you if they don't perceive you as a threat. No one can stop you if no one knows what you are doing.

In this situation, sensitivity, secrecy, and flexibility are assets. Cannily make use of them and you will succeed.

35. OPHELIA'S GHOST

You have been used, ignored, marginalized, or otherwise mistreated. Acknowledge this, be compassionate with yourself, and take steps to heal. Feel your painful feelings, but also believe in your ability to triumph.

In Shakespeare's *Hamlet*, Ophelia is a melancholy beauty who could have evolved into a powerful wisewoman had she not died from a broken heart at far too young an age.

Here, Ophelia's ghost, unseen by mortal eyes, is calmly watching Hamlet talk with his friend Horatio and the gravediggers who are even now digging her grave.

In life, Ophelia loved Hamlet, who was so wrapped up in his own problems and prejudices, he wasn't inclined to reciprocate, although he had no qualms about using her and then casting her aside. Now, while the insult still smarts, the fog of illusion has cleared, and she can see Hamlet as the narcissist he is.

Even more importantly, her own true self is coming into focus. She realizes she is—and, in fact, has always been—powerful, beautiful, and infinitely worthy of love.

While Ophelia is generally seen as a tragic figure, here we see hope. For while she has changed forms, she is still here. And while the skulls symbolize the part of her that has perished, the butterflies mirror her transformation into her limitless and ethereal form.

Every life contains heartbreak and hurt. While it may be tempting to close your heart or harden it against the world, don't. Breathe into the pain and let it inspire your personal evolution. Let go of your old visions, dreams, and expectations to discover even better ones. Inhabit your infinite identity, spread your newfound wings, and fly.

Clarity, healing, and renewal are available to you now. Like Ophelia's grave and the butterfly's cocoon, this is a portal of transformation. Transcend the limited illusion of who you thought you were and become the unlimited being you are.

36. PUMPKIN BABY

*You have conceived of something magical.
You are about to bring forth a beautiful new being, condition,
or project. Prepare for a profound and positive change.*

This card could indicate a pregnancy, but it could also be that you are about to adopt a child, birth a creative project, take home an animal friend, or otherwise hold the space for something wonderful and new to come through. Whatever it is, angels and beings of light surround you, tirelessly praying for you, blessing your birthing process, and sending love to your (symbolic or literal) baby.

Bringing in something new is a sacred sort of alchemy. Consider planting a seed. First you wait, then you begin to see a sprout, and eventually, with the help of nature and the Great Mystery, there is a plant where once there was only bare ground. In time, the plant blossoms and bears fruit. Every fruit contains its own seeds, each with potential for new life. In time, that life will express itself wildly, generously, and in countless variations.

This supernatural mother-to-be is pleased, but she is also intimidated. If you feel that way too, you are not alone. Births and significant changes always come along with worries and fears. These feelings prove that you care and are approaching the gestation and incubation process with appropriate seriousness, attention, and respect.

You can minimize your fears and magnify your joy when you listen deeply to your body's wisdom and the whispers of the angels. Nourish and care for yourself: body, mind, and spirit. Eat healthy food. Exercise gently. Get plenty of sleep. Embellish the nursery or gather and organize the creative and practical tools you need. Wisely and conscientiously prepare for what is to come.

This is a happy new change that will transform your life forever. Nurture it, make way for it, welcome it, and step proudly into your important new role.

37. IMMORTAL GAZE

*Pause and observe. With unwavering patience, listen deeply
and watch closely before you form a conclusion or make a move.
The true nature of a person or situation will reveal itself in time,
providing you with the information you need.*

Here we have a shrewd vampire faerie who has seen it all. Her immortality means she has no sense of urgency. She has learned that most folks will show you who and what they are if you simply gaze at them unflinchingly, unapologetically, and for an extended stretch of time.

This card indicates you must not blindly trust someone, rush into something, or take a situation at face value.

Sometimes, you must read the fine print, and if it crosses your mind that something is 'too good to be true', that may indeed be the case.

On the other hand, in time, you may discover that the object of your inquiry is indeed trustworthy. In this case, too, your patience and caution will be rewarded. For with due diligence, you need not simply wonder and hope for the best. By doing your homework, you will have actual data points supporting your decision to move forward, collaborate, or commit.

There is a myth that your intuition will always reveal everything to you right away. In fact, when divine timing is at work, there are no clear or obvious answers right out of the gate. These are moments when you must get comfortable with uncertainty and to let go of the need to immediately see your next step.

A wisewoman knows many things, including that she doesn't always know.

Embrace the ambiguity. If you don't know what to do, don't do anything other than calmly observe. Bide your time and see what is revealed. You will know when the time is right to act.

38. PUMPKIN THIEF

*You need not forage, steal, or scrounge for money, approval, or love.
You deserve the best and are far more capable than you know.
Change your paradigm from one of lack to one of plenty and expect
an endless stream of wealth in all its many forms.*

This adorable little pumpkin thief has been skulking around a barren wasteland, looking for pumpkins that are not hers to take. She hasn't yet discovered that she holds the power to make her own pumpkins grow in profusion, at an accelerated rate, on any soil and at any time of year. Once realizing her true identity and the magic within, she can cease her habits of snatching and hoarding, opting instead to relax and revel in the boundless power to receive.

You too have been operating under an illusion. You have believed that you do not deserve unconditional love and support, that what you desire is hard to come by, or that wealth is for other people, but not for you.

This is a clear message to change your inner narrative. Love is not outside of you. You are love. You deserve wealth, success, sweetness, joy, beauty, and all other favorable conditions, which are already part of you. Find them within you. Feel grateful for them. Place your awareness on them. This will magnify and turn up the brightness on all the many blessings that are yours to enjoy.

This could also be a message about generosity, for when you know you are endlessly blessed, giving is easier and more natural. Conversely, the more you lovingly give, the more you actualize the reality that you are endlessly blessed. What you send out will gather momentum and return to you in waves.

Always remember that having more does not equate to being greedy, for love is endless, and the more bounty you receive, the more you have to give.

Claim your divine inheritance and birthright. Know that you deserve it all. This will open you up to your boundless supply of every wonderful thing.

39. WILL-O'-THE-WISP

39. WILL-O'-THE-WISP

Follow the spark of your inspiration.
The Universe is sending you signs and lighting your way.
Pay attention to opportunities, and act as you are guided.

Here we have a sweet, little bioluminescent faerie witch on the sacred isle of Avalon. She is holding an enchanted jack-o'-lantern to serve as a guiding light that will navigate you through the mist.

Nature and the Goddess desire to help you with the object of your inquiry or the central issue at hand. And, in fact, they have already been offering you this support. Notice the guidance you're currently receiving and acknowledge the divine nudges you've already received.

One way the Universe speaks to you is through your authentic desires: the dreams, goals, and wishes that fill you with joy and a sense of expansion. Even if you can't see the whole path, you can still look for your next step. It will be illuminated by the emotion of excitement and the whispered promise of adventure and fun.

Furthermore, don't ignore synchronicities. For example, symbols, words, numbers, animals, or animal imagery that you see multiple times in succession are like ethereal lights in the fog, showing you the way.

Don't overlook 'coincidences' and unusual opportunities. For example, after you do a love spell, a friend might invite you to a painting class, where you meet a handsome new love interest. Or, after getting your resume ready for your dream job, you could 'randomly' run into an old friend, who, it turns out, knows just the position for you.

This will-o'-the-wisp is beckoning you toward a new level of success. Even though this is a positive transition, it may still feel scary because it contains so many unknowns. But rest assured: your guidance is steering you right.

Invoke even more divine support, follow the faerie lights, and you will soon find yourself in a beautiful new realm.

40. JACK-O'-LANTERN OF LOVE

Take comfort in your friends and loved ones. Let everyday moments of connection warm your heart. Affectionate togetherness will temper your melancholy and keep your worries at bay.

This sweet little witch is highly sensitive by nature and has been no stranger to feeling generally anxious, or worried about being odd or out of place. That's why she's basking in the happy glow of the jack-o'-lantern of love, an immortal pumpkin spirit who emanates the inextinguishable warmth of friendship's everlasting glow.

Similarly, you must draw upon the loving support of others now. Our culture is overly fixated on values—such as wealth, success, and attractiveness—that ultimately prove hollow when you have no one to share them with. While there is nothing wrong with these, none of them will bring you joy on their own, and all of them pale in comparison to the more lasting and authentic joy of simply having a friend.

Rekindle an old friendship, make a new one, or reach out to friends and family members who are in your life now. Instead of sending a text, consider making a phone call, or writing a letter on paper and putting it in the actual mail. Or schedule a lunch date, host a get together, plan a friends' trip, or get a plane ticket to visit one or more members of your family.

While there are certainly times when it's appropriate to end a friendship, be honest with yourself: are you nursing a petty grudge more attentively than you're nourishing the more enduring qualities of companionship, compassion, and care?

It's natural to worry about whether other people love and approve of you, but remember that others also worry about the same things. We're all perfectly imperfect, and most often, no matter what has happened in the past, friends and family will be honored and touched when you reach out to them and show them positive regard.

Tend to your little sparks of connection, regularly, and keep the fire of friendship burning. In the darkest night, even one single candle flame of love will confer a glorious glow.

41. MEDUSA'S MYSTERIES

*Call upon the protection of the Great Goddess.
Find power in your feminine aspects. Embody your fierceness,
heal old pain, and be unapologetic about wielding
your authority and letting your beauty shine.*

Medusa was a gorgeous sea spirit known as a gorgon. After catching the eye of the god Poseidon, he chased her down and attacked her while she was attempting to find sanctuary in Athena's temple. Athena, ostensibly, did not approve of such things happening in her temple, so she transformed Medusa into serpent-haired monster whose gaze would instantly turn men into stone. As if that weren't enough, Athena then sent the hero Perseus to kill her.

On the surface, this is a tale of a god, and then a goddess, and then a famed hero behaving unforgivably. But on a deeper level, it is a sacred women's mystery. It whispers to us through the centuries, reminding us that we can draw upon Medusa's fierceness. We can wield our magic, heal our trauma, and transcend the effects of mistreatment and shame.

For Athena's identity is inextricably and alchemically interwoven with Medusa's, and Medusa's beheading transformed her into a goddess in her own right. So, was Athena enraged at Medusa (as is generally assumed), or was she enraged on Medusa's behalf, and so granted her an initiation that would confer great power upon not just Medusa, but also all of womankind?

Make friends with your body and its cycles: your menses, fertility, reproductive organs, hormone fluctuations, and all the many changes and shades of experience such things confer in various ways, throughout your life.

And, be fierce: call upon the Goddess and refuse to be captured, intimidated, overpowered, or tamed. Say what you need to say, protect yourself as needed, and set boundaries as you desire.

Even though, in the past, you may have believed your body, sensitivity, emotions, or feminine aspects were something to hide or apologize for, the opposite is true. These things are in fact your allies. Work with them now to manifest your triumph and success.

42. PUMPKIN PROMISE

The Universe is gifting you with precisely what you desire. But you won't receive it all at once. You will unlock your life's most ideal flow when you cultivate gratitude, lovingly nurture the seeds of happiness, and focus on all the blessings you already have.

This lovely witch is handing you everything you ever wished and hoped for in your innermost heart of hearts. The unwise would feel slighted by the tininess of the pumpkin in which this gift appears, comparing its volume to the abundance of larger pumpkins in her midst. But with your love, care, and grateful attention, this tiny pumpkin will expand into prolific and countless crops in its own divine timing.

If you try to rush through your fairytale to get to your happily-ever-after, you are missing the point. Life is not a finite timeline, but an endless kaleidoscope and tumbling fountain of light.

When you desire something, you don't simply want the result but all the expansion you encounter along your way. As you go, you will meet lovely people, learn important lessons, and revel in the preciousness of the everyday moments of your life.

You may think you desire ease, but seeming roadblocks will be vital to your happiness and success. You may believe you prefer directness, but U-turns will turn out to offer insights you otherwise couldn't have gained.

There will always be those who are more accomplished than you, and more talented or attractive by the standards of the day. This is true for everyone. And yet it is also true that no two people are alike, and we all have something unique and special to share. Competing and comparing will only serve to distract you from your goal. More importantly, you will miss out on all the joy available now and at every stage along your way.

Receive the gift of the Universe as it is offered. Cultivate gratitude. Look for satisfaction and delight in each moment, and you will find it.

43. MOON MISTRESS

Connect with your wildness. Find your freedom. Make peace with your magical identity and harmonize your inner and outer worlds.

This divine female is the full moon incarnate, petting her beloved werewolf devotees. Far from violent, terrible, or out-of-control, these shape-shifting canines are at peace. For it is only when they try to suppress their own nature that they express that nature in a volatile or dangerous way.

The moon mistress has appeared to help you admit and make friends with a vital aspect of who you are. She sees that you've ignored or denied a natural desire or need. While discipline can certainly be helpful at times, some proclivities must not be repressed, for they are not bad habits or shameful yearnings, but fundamental features of your divine and beautiful self.

This could be a message to fully claim and take pride in your gender, sexuality, heritage, or spirituality. Or it could be a nudge to express your creative cravings or admit your need for adventure and change.

In what ways are you hiding who you are to make others comfortable, or to fit into an externally imposed ideal? What fear is holding you back from what you would really like to try? What judgment is locking you away from the transformative and freeing light of the moon?

It could be that your culture or family expects you to take a particular path in life, when in fact it doesn't feel authentic to you. Not everyone needs to do things in a specific order or certain way. Some conventions will resonate with you and others won't. And the only person who knows what is right for you is you.

Once you connect with, and appropriately express, the fullness of who you are, you will find peace.

Align with the light of the moon. Listen to the intrinsic desires of your body, mind, emotions, and heart. Dance wildly and run with the wolves. Above all, be free.

44. AUTUMN ANGEL

*Be still. Connect with the radiant beauty at your heart.
When you embody divine peace, you will be a light and comfort
to others and call beautiful conditions into your world.*

This is Gabriella, the angel of autumn, meditating tranquilly in the Halloween sunrise. These adorable young cat siblings sensed her presence. They gathered around her to bask in her sweet and loving energy, and everyone is just as pleased and satisfied as possible.

If you have been rushing around frantically, trying to force something to happen, or attempting to change a condition that is out of your control, this is a message to stop. Take a step back, relax, and connect with silence and space. Perhaps take a bath, gaze at the sunrise, or arrange for a solitary retreat. Then, realign with divinity. Call on angels or other manifestations of spirit. Return to your heart and to your heart-centered intentions. This will bring about the inner shift that will allow things to flow ideally and with ease.

Cats like to settle around those who sit quietly and emanate peace. Similarly, your most generative life conditions will not come to you if you are constantly on the chase. There are times when you must find contentment with where you already are. For like attracts like, and contentment draws more contentment unto itself.

The alchemy of manifestation is a delicate balance: just as you must exhale to inhale, you must balance your action with relaxation and your single-minded focus with a clear and steady inner calm.

Too much action can cause us to forget the love that motivated our goals in the first place. So, sometimes we must stop and recharge by quietly soaking in the soft light of compassion and universal love.

Take a break. Be kind to yourself. Follow your intuition about gentle self-care practices that will help you to rediscover your guidance and realign with your heart. And the cats of good fortune will surely cozy up to you and make themselves at home.

45. DRACULA'S HEIRESS

An inheritance of great value is on the horizon for you. You are literally coming into money, or another precious gift is being passed down or handed to you, such as a role, a talent, or a cache of valuable resources. Accept this with gratitude and vow to be a responsible steward of what you receive.

This is Dracula's grandniece, the sole heir of his fortune and legacy. Her dragonling companion is an ancient creature: a loyal friend, familiar, and symbol of the power and authority of this ancestral line. Dracula's heiress doesn't question her right to all she has inherited, for she must concentrate on her obligation to rule conscientiously and wisely manage her wealth.

Follow this example now. We all have our paths to walk and our parts to play in the drama of this earthly existence. Don't worry about your worthiness, for it's never wise to refuse the gifts meant for you. Even if you don't feel perfectly prepared, you must be willing to learn as you go.

If you're unsure what this card refers to, look closely at what is already present in your life while also looking out for what is to come. It's possible that you are about to be promoted or to receive an unexpected blessing or boon. Expect some sort of invitation to take on a sacred duty or to level up in one or more important ways. Or recognize such an invitation that you have already received.

You may possess a creative, psychic, or practical gift that has been passed down to you from your ancestors, conferred upon you by a teacher, or gleaned from formative experiences in your past.

Accept the talent, gift, role, or fortune that is indeed yours to claim. Honestly assess all the many responsibilities that come along with it. And take pride in being the best heir or heiress you can be.

46. DAUGHTERS OF NIGHT

Beautiful blessings are on their way to you — say yes to them. Creative inspiration, happiness, and luxury are flowing to you and through you in endless waves. Relax, receive, and be glad.

Say hello to the Three Graces: divine attendants to the goddess Aphrodite, and daughters of Nyx, the goddess of night. In the center is Aglaia, whose name means 'the wonderful'. On the left is Thalia, whose name means 'plenty'. And on the right is Euphrosyne, whose name means 'joy'. The Graces are offering you a profusion of presents. They want you to receive with gratitude and grace, for this will allow them to continue to bestow their boundless gifts.

If the affluence of the Graces is not immediately apparent to you, it is because you must shift from tension and worry to leisure and ease. While it can be challenging to manage this when you appear to be experiencing struggle or lack, you must, nonetheless, cultivate an attitude of trust. You can start with one simple action, such as taking a walk in nature, soaking in a warm bath, or making a list of all the beautiful blessings you already have. Then, continue: gently, incrementally, relax your body and swing your attention away from lack.

Look into the Graces' beautiful eyes. Gaze at their ancient faces. Take in all the many symbols of infinity piled before them. Breathe, unclench, and let yourself open up to the gifts the Graces and the Goddess are yearning to bequeath.

If you are asking about a financial opportunity, business venture, friendship, or romance, the Graces are saying 'yes'. They see great potential in this prospect and fully expect you to thrive when you move forward and zestfully seize the day.

The appearance of the Graces is a positive omen indeed. Just as Halloween is a time to revel in sweet and abundant bounty of the earth, now is a time for you to smile, relax, and savor the harvest's delectable fruit.

ABOUT THE AUTHOR

Tess Whitehurst believes life is magical. In addition to authoring this deck, she's the author of *The Oracle of Portals*, *Cosmic Dancer Oracle*, *The Queen Mab Oracle*, *The Magic of Flowers Oracle*, and *The Angel Magic Oracle*.

Tess's books include the bestselling *Magical Housekeeping*, the award-winning *The Magic of Flowers*, and lots of other fan favorites such as *The Self-Love Superpower*, *You Are Magical*, *The Good Energy Book*, and *The Magic of Trees*. Articles she has written have appeared in *Writer's Digest*, *Spirit & Destiny*, and *Llewellyn's Magical Almanac*. She has appeared on morning shows on both Fox and NBC, and her feng shui work was featured on the Bravo TV show *Flipping Out*.

Tess's teachings about magic and spirituality appear extensively online, particularly on her website, TessWhitehurst.com, and via her online membership portal, *Wisdom Circle Online School of Magical Arts*.

Tess lives in the Rocky Mountains of Colorado with a handsome man and a handsome cat. Visit Tess and sign up for her free newsletter at **TessWhitehurst.com**.   Photo credit: Whitney DeVoto

ABOUT THE ARTIST

Jasmine Becket-Griffith is a traditional acrylic painter who combines elements of realism, fantasy, and the surreal. In her creations, historical and spiritual references are intertwined with fairytales and the beauty of nature. Her trademark liquid-eyed maidens evoke a wide range of emotions and responses to the surrounding imagery.

Jasmine lives in Long Beach, California and spends her time between her secondary studios in Julian, California, and Kansas City. Jasmine was born in Kansas and began her professional art career in 1997. While usually painting or traveling, she enjoys spending time with her partner David Van Gough, co-creator of the *Death & the Maiden*™ universe, her solo creative brand *Strangeling*™, her association with the *Walt Disney* company, playing with her cats, nature, travel, and plant-based cooking.

To learn more about Jasmine and her work, visit ***www.strangeling.com***.

For more information on this or
any Blue Angel Publishing© release,
please visit our website at:

www.blueangelonline.com